DEDICATION

To all Eicoff employees, past and present, who turned Alvin Eicoff's vision into reality, creating one of the world's best and most successful advertising agencies. To honor the agency and Al, all proceeds from this book will be donated to the Off the Street Club

INTRODUCTION

This is a love story. I loved Alvin Eicoff, who was my boss and mentor and made my career possible. I also loved his genius—I have never met anyone who was so brilliant. It's fair to assert that advertising would not be what it is today without his contributions.

And I loved many of his idiosyncrasies, which is probably too kind a word to describe some of his behaviors. Al was capable of doing and saying anything. Sometimes what came out of his mouth was pure genius. And sometimes, it was pure baloney. In either case, he was never dull, and he made each work day an adventure.

To be fair, I didn't love everything about Al. At times, he could be obstinate. He'd get an idea in his head and nothing could dislodge it, no matter how wrong it might have been. He could make me crazy with his mule-headedness, and he could offend people because he had no filter—he was not a particularly self-aware person.

Nonetheless, I absolutely believe that Al deserves this "book"—I put the word in quotes because its page length is small relative to most books. But it contains a lot of big ideas and stories about larger-than-life characters. My fear has always been that if I don't write this book, these ideas and stories will be lost. Everyone knows the giants in the advertising business—David Ogilvy, Leo Burnett and Mary Wells to name a few. But not everyone knows Al. He operated largely in the television direct response arena rather than in more mainstream advertising circles.

It's also due to his appearance. If you saw Al walking down the street for the first time, you'd guess that he was a used car salesman. He wore loud, mismatched, food-stained clothes, topped by a toupee that was sometimes askew. For much of his life, he was at least 50 pounds overweight. When he spoke, his voice sounded like sandpaper, and if he was particularly enthusiastic about a point, you might get some of his spit on your suit. He was as far from *Mad Men's* Don Draper as you can get, bearing no resemblance to the prototypical advertising genius.

And it's also due to who he was. As I noted, Al didn't have a filter, and so he made enemies. For years, the Direct Marketing Association Hall of Fame refused to admit him despite his huge contributions—some people didn't want to see him honored in any way because he had offended them. The late George Lazarus, the *Chicago Tribune* marketing columnist, refused to speak to him for years. People had trouble seeing past his surface behaviors and recognizing his incredible advertising insights and innovations.

Those insights and innovations include: introducing and establishing the 800 number as a response vehicle; creating key outlet marketing (later called trade support advertising) that translated direct response techniques into retail-focused commercials; pioneering media buying and creative tactics that have become standard operating procedure in the business; making a television commercial in which he coaxed an elephant onto a pool table.

Okay, that last one might not qualify as "insight" or "innovation", but it shows you how far he would go to sell a product.

I'm going to tell you about Al by telling stories about him. There are a lot of stories. Funny stories, poignant stories, stories about the business. And stories that reveal his complexities and contradictions.

For instance, in 1981 when Ogilvy expressed interest in purchasing A. Eicoff & Company, he called my extension and asked me to come into his office. This phone call was not his style—if he had something to tell you, he usually barged into your office and said what he had to say. So I knew this must be a serious matter. When I entered, he asked me to close the door.

"You're now the president of the agency," he said.

I was stunned and didn't know what to say.

"Ogilvy won't buy us until management is in place. So you're the president."

I walked out of his office in a daze. It wasn't just that I was now going to be head of the agency. It meant that Al was on his way out. Clearly, though, he didn't realize it.

Later, I talked to him about it. "Al, this is going to be great for me and terrible for you."

"Nah, they'll figure out how smart I am and make me chairman of the board, you'll see."

How could he not perceive that he didn't fit in the Ogilvy culture? At the time, David Ogilvy told people that he wanted the agency to be staffed by "gentlemen with brains." Al had the brains, but he did not always act like a gentleman. His rough edges were too rough for the Ogilvy culture.

But he was oblivious to this truth. He was sure they would recognize his genius and give him significant responsibilities. Later, I'll describe the fallout when he realized that this was not going to be the case.

For now, though, consider what this brief story suggests. Al was someone who over 20 years ago proclaimed that in the future, advertising would be a direct response world. He took in what was happening back then—the experiments with interactive television, the birth of the internet, the new technologies being tested—and saw that at some point, people wouldn't just be calling 800 numbers but would have other, technologically-based response options.

How could someone with that much foresight lack the insight to see that he didn't fit in Ogilvy's culture?

That's just one of the questions about Al that this book will explore. Let's start exploring it with the story of how the son of a general store owner in Lewiston, Montana came to Chicago in the '50s and started an ad agency.

Chapter 1—AN IRON WILL IN THE GOLDEN AGE OF ADVERTISING

Al took a long and winding path to become the head of a Chicago ad agency, a path that started in his home town of Lewiston, Montana. He grew up the son of a shopkeeper, spending his free time fishing in mountain-fed streams. A good student, he started college at Stanford University and later transferred to the University of Texas, where he majored in accounting. After graduating, he joined the Army and was stationed in Germany where he was a reporter for the military's *Stars and Stripes* newspaper.

At first glance, none of this might seem to have prepared Al for an advertising career. But if you think about it, his accounting background helped him learn how to run a profitable business; his newspaper work enabled him to hone his writing, a skill that was essential early on when Al wrote many of the agency's commercials; and Al believed that growing up in a small town helped him relate to television viewers who were "regular people", a quality he claimed Leo Burnett also shared because of his small-town upbringing as the son of a shopkeeper.

After his army service, Al went to New York and his friend, Mel Moore, fixed him up with Helene, who became his wife when she was 18 and Al was 22. Shortly thereafter, they moved back to Lewiston where Al got a job as both a reporter and ad salesman for the local newspaper. Helene, though, hated it there. A native New Yorker, she issued an ultimatum: "I can't live here; I want to return to New York. If you want to stay, fine, but I'm leaving." Al left with her and briefly worked selling radio time for stations in New York. Then his company transferred him to Chicago, and that's where the real Al Eicoff story begins.

THE GENIUS OF A PLAIN BROWN WRAPPER

When Al arrived in Chicago to sell radio time, he was working with a company called dCon, which made a product that was essentially rat poison. Al convinced the owner, Lee Ratner (yes, that was his real name), to start running commercials on the 50,000 watt stations he represented, but he made a suggestion: Create brown paper packaging and advertise that dCon comes in a plain brown paper wrapper. Al grasped that people wanted to get rid of their rodent problem but didn't want their neighbors to know they had one. If dCon arrived on doorsteps with this nondescript packaging, people wouldn't hesitate to buy the product.

The strategy worked and Lee Ratner was so impressed that he hired Al. Lee was a classic wheeler dealer, the type of person who'd try to sell you swamp land in Florida (which was actually one of the schemes in which he involved Al). When Al talked about Lee, the most common adjective he used was "crazy". Once, he and Al were in a busy Florida restaurant and they were sitting in a booth for a few minutes without a waiter stopping at their table to take an order. Lee stood up, pulled out a handful of hundred dollar bills and tossed them high in the air, asking, "Can we get some service here?" They got some service.

The culture at dCon was also crazy. The environment was about having fun as much as it was about work, and Al loved having fun. The company was looking for other products that might duplicate dCon's success, and one day a guy walked through their doors with a product he claimed could grow hair. Lee was about to depart on a two-week vacation, but before he left, he instructed their CFO, a guy named Harold who was completely bald, to try the product to see if it worked. When Lee returned, he was talking with Al about various matters when he recalled that Harold had tried the hair restoring product, and he asked Al to get him and see the results. Harold walked into the office wearing a hat, and Lee told him to take it off. Lo and behold, Harold had a full head of hair.

Lee jumped out of his chair, waved his hands in the air and shouted, "We're rich, we're rich!"

Finally, Al admitted that Harold was wearing a toupee that Al had bought.

Lee also paid Al a crazy salary for those days: $50,000. In exchange, he treated Al like a slave. Al was on the golf course when Lee sent him a message that he wanted Al at the airport and on a plane within an hour. Al called Lee and said he was in the middle of a golf game. Lee said he didn't care, just get on that plane.

More than once when I talked with Al about his time at dCon, Al said that Lee owned him 24 hours a day. It was a terrible feeling and one that Al never forgot. A number of years later, shortly after I joined A. Eicoff & Company, I would stay after 5:00 to get work done. One evening, Al was still at the office—not working, but playing gin rummy with his cronies. He said, "Go home. Don't make the same mistake I did (when working for Lee Ratner)." It was no coincidence that few people at Eicoff ever worked past 5:00 or on weekends. Unlike just about every other ad agency, employees worked normal hours, based on Al's belief that spending too much of your life at work was no life at all.

In 1956 or 1957, Lee sold dCon, and Al was out of a job. He was living an affluent lifestyle, residing in Glencoe and a member of the country club. It was a lifestyle he couldn't afford if he didn't figure out a way to make money.

CREATING AN AD AGENCY UNLIKE ANY OTHER

The advertising agency business was a natural fit for Al. After all, he understood the business from a number of angles—as an advertiser, a writer, a media rep—and the early fifties was a time when a lot of ad agencies were getting started. Initially, he recruited old pal Mel Moore and another guy to form Moore, Gottschalk and Eicoff. It was a rough period, and perhaps inevitably, Al broke away from his two partners and opened A. Eicoff & Co. in 1957.

At first, his clients were mostly homebuilders and the vast majority of his billing was radio. It was a struggle, and even though Al moved from Glencoe to a condo on Lake Shore Drive, he was barely keeping his head above water.

Then one day, a guy came to his agency with a product called Tarn-X, a tarnish remover. It became a client and started to sell, but when the company owner couldn't pay his bills, Al took him to court and received the company in the settlement. Shortly thereafter, he met Manny Gutterman. Short and squat, Manny was the

12th child of 12, and he was the only boy. He was also a character out of Damon Runyon—to say his language was colorful is an understatement. Al did the advertising, Manny got the distribution, and together, they started to make a little money. Their concept—first known as key outlet marketing and later referred to as trade support advertising—was brilliant. The commercials drove people to stores in search of the advertised products, and the stores, because they were featured in the commercials, gave the products terrific shelf placement and space.

Al's big break came, though, when he met Sy Sanders of Columbia Records. This was a major account—their offers included album collections of well-known classical music, big band hits and so on. It remains a mystery how Al was able to secure a major account at this early stage of his career, but Al was an entrepreneur at heart, and he was already adept at figuring out what to say and do to attract new business.

But what he was also learning was how to adapt. Before 1960, no length limits were imposed on commercials. They could be as long or as short as was necessary to make an effective pitch. Early on, Al brought pitchmen from the Atlantic City boardwalk and Chicago's Maxwell Street, placed them in front of the camera and had them do their pitches, and some of these spots were program-length. These really were the first infomercials, but long-form spots came to an abrupt end with Federal Communication Commission Chairman Newton Minow's "Vast Wasteland" speech—the one in which he declared television a vast wasteland and began imposing restrictions designed to improve quality. One of these restrictions involved limiting commercials to no more than two minutes in length.

At first, Al and others thought this spelled the end to their business. How do you create motivating commercials when you lack sufficient time to do so? How do you get all the demonstrations, benefits and ordering information in a short form commercial, especially when the offer requires explanation?

But Al adapted and became a master of the two-minute form. While other agencies moved to 30-second spots as the standard length, Al often used the maximum amount of time available to create the most effective spots possible. Back then, Al wrote many of the agency's spots, and he wrote them fast and often nailed them on the first try. Through experience and instinct, he knew what it took to compel viewers to act—to pick up the phone and order or to drive to the store.

And his efforts paid off. Not only were Columbia Records and Tarn-X making money, but Hair Wiz (a do-it-yourself hair-cutting product) was also selling. And then the agency picked up an account called Donatelli Honey and Egg Crème Facial, and that's where I entered the picture.

FROM DOUBT TO TRUE BELIEF

I had not yet joined Rhodes Pharmacal, the marketer of the Donatelli product, but I was friends with the company owner's son, Jim Rose, and he asked me to sit in on a meeting with him, Al and others. I was working at the Edward H. Weiss agency at the time, and Jim wanted to know what I thought of Al's methods. In the beginning, I was skeptical about everything I heard about the agency and Al's theories. Weiss was a traditional ad agency, and I worked on accounts like Wishbone Salad Dressing, Sara Lee and WBBM. As a result, I was accustomed to media buys that relied on rating points and frequency measures.

I became even more skeptical when I attended the meeting with Jim; it was like walking into a corner saloon filled with tough guys and lunatics. I entered Al's office, and it was difficult to see who was there at first because it was filled with smoke—everyone was puffing on cigarettes. As the tobacco cloud cleared, I observed Manny Gutterman and his two sons talking on speaker phone with Mort, a Gray Drugs executive. Mort was shouting, "Put that stuff on the plane, we can't keep it in stock!" Manny was screaming back about inventory and trying to negotiate a better price.

Shortly thereafter, I joined Rhodes Pharmacal as a vice president, and I began working closely with Al and his agency. I couldn't believe the low rates that Al was getting for the spots, and I sent copies of the rates to my friend, Phil Gerber, who was a top media executive at J. Walter Thompson, and he said there was no way Al could get those rates.

So I challenged Al, demanding to see affidavits from the stations verifying the rates. For the first six months, I was a skeptic. But Al and I would discuss and debate and eventually, I became a believer. I realized he was on to something that no one else in the business got. It took me a while to unlearn what I had been taught, but once I accepted what Al was telling me, there was no going back.

For that reason, when Al offered me a job as a senior vice president in charge of new business, I accepted. Not that I didn't have reservations. But I took the job for a number of reasons. First, I believed in Al and his advertising theories. Second, I anticipated that I would be out of a job soon. Donatelli Honey and Egg Crème Facial contained a preservative system that they decided to change—they reformulated the product using formaldehyde. A big mistake, since I began getting calls complaining that the product was hard enough that you could play handball with it. I had two small children at the time and I worried that I would soon be unemployed, making Al's offer more attractive than it might have been otherwise.

But third, and most importantly, my wife, Linda, told me she trusted Al. Linda was more perceptive about people than most, and if her gut told her that Al was a man of his word, I figured I could bet our future on that instinct.

The way Al offered me a job is worth describing, since it will give you a sense of the agency at the time as well as Al's salesmanship. We were meeting about Rhodes, which was going down the tubes and owed Al money, when he told me that he had received a call from a U.S. Senator about handling his campaign advertising, but that he needed to find someone younger and more polished than anyone at the agency who could work effectively with the Senator. Did I know anyone who might fit the bill?

Now, I'm not sure how truthful this story was. It's possible that Al improvised on the spot, recognizing that I might be open to a job offer but that a direct approach might scare me off. No doubt, he also worried that if he poached me, Rhodes wouldn't pay Al the money they owed him. So he floated the story about the Senator as a trial balloon, or at least that's my suspicion.

I told him I might be interested. Though the Senator never became a client, the subject of my working for Al had been broached and began to gain momentum. It's possible that Al worked out a deal with Rhodes to reduce the amount they owed him in exchange for securing their permission to hire me.

But that wasn't the only tricky issue involved in my hiring. Al's problem was that his two key people, Bob Berg and Jerry Siegel, felt threatened by me. Al needed to find a way to justify hiring me. So while I was still at Rhodes, he had me accompany him on a new business call. We secured a small piece of business, and he had the justification he needed to offer me a job.

THE WILD MIDWEST

It was even crazier than I could have imagined. I had been accustomed to highly professional, buttoned-down work environments. There was nothing buttoned down about A. Eicoff & Co. In those days, its staff was straight out of central casting. It went beyond the drinking and card playing. Al hired one person whose qualifications for the job were that he was Al's sister's Arthur Murray dance instructor. He also hired Sonny Delmonico, his sister's hairdresser. The head of research welcomed me to the agency by inviting me into his office and showing me the handgun he kept in his desk drawer. Fortunately, the agency's radio/media director had left by the time I arrived—he had the unfortunate habit of running schedules without client approval. He almost put the agency out of business before Al figured out what he was doing and fired him.

Al didn't like to fire people. Despite Al's coarse exterior, he was fiercely loyal to just about everyone he hired and couldn't bring himself to fire anyone, even if they were incompetent.

My main impression from my initial months at the agency, though, was that Al created an environment conducive to craziness; it kept things from getting boring. For instance, Al called me into Bob Berg's office and introduced me to a guy named Lee Weiner who he said was the "inventor of the aerosol can." This may have been true, half-true or completely false—you never quite knew with Al. He had a product that Al described as "hot cold cream" that you squirted out of an aerosol can.

"What do you think?" he asked me.

"Well, what does it do?"

"Put out your hands and I'll show you."

I cupped my hands and Al blasted a huge spray of hot cold cream that rebounded off my hands into my face. Thinking that Al was playing a practical joke, I grabbed the can from him and started to spray him with the stuff, and he leapt up and began running down the hallway and I chased him, trying to nail him with the hot cold cream. As he's running, he's yelling back at me to stop, that this isn't a joke, the guy is for real. We return to Bob Berg's office, both of us looking like the topping for an ice cream sundae. Lee Weiner stares at us like we've taken leave of our senses, grabs the can from us and backs slowly out of the room, saying, "I think I'll go now." We lost the prospective client, but it didn't matter—we knew there were a lot more clients out there.

Al was unpredictable; you never knew what he might do or say. We had a client for whom we had just run test spots, and they hadn't worked. He asked me to join him in a meeting with this client to talk about why it had failed. I asked him what he was going to say to them, and he shrugged and said, "I'll think of something." We walked into the meeting and there were four guys in suits, looking like they wanted an explanation.

We sat down and Al said, "I think you guys are in the wrong business, you should be selling guitars."

Whether Al was trying to defuse the tension in the meeting with a non sequitur or he just said the first thing that popped into his head, I don't know. But Al said it like it was an eminently sensible explanation for their commercial's failure.

All this isn't to say that Al was all fun and no business. In fact, a day rarely went by when he didn't ask me, "Bring in any new business today?" For six months, I couldn't respond affirmatively. Yet to Al's credit, he never made me feel like my job was at risk. For someone who was impulsive and flew by the seat of his pants, he could also be remarkably patient.

His patience paid off when after six months, I brought in three accounts in one week: TV Magic Cards,

Dark Eyes/Long Nails and Texative (a division of Sunbeam). Those first two accounts may sound sketchy by the agency's standards today, but back then, they provided the type of billings the agency needed; Dark Eyes/Long Nails was the agency's biggest client for a number of years, billing $5 million annually (a significant amount in the '60s/70s).

You would think that Al would bend over backwards to be nice to his largest account, but if you think that, you didn't know Al. The company was owned by a grandmotherly woman named Charlotte Barth—no one used her first name, she was Mrs. Barth to one and all. Her sales rep, who later became her partner, was Herman Goldenberg; Herman was the one who helped me get my foot in the door.

Al knew all this, of course, but that didn't stop him from insulting Herman in our first meeting with the client. He told Mrs. Barth, "You've got the wrong sales rep; you need to get Pete Pankow." Herman was outraged, and he asked me how in the world Alvin could say this given that Herman was the one who helped us get the account. Then as now, I had no answer for Al's sometimes inexplicable behaviors.

Shortly thereafter, Mrs. Barth and Herman were in my office for a meeting and Alvin walked in, asked me a question and then left without even acknowledging his largest client. Mrs. Barth turned to me and said, "How much money do we have to spend before he says hello? I'm afraid I'm going to have to rethink our relationship."

Fearful that we were about to lose the account, I rushed into Al's office.

"What did you do?" I asked, incredulous that he could have offended our largest client.

"I was busy," he said, as if that were an excuse.

I told him that he had to repair things, and he said okay. I scheduled a dinner near the airport for the four of us, and before the meeting, I asked that he just be nice to them.

We sat down, and within seconds, Al began telling jokes so dirty that even I was offended. I was sure that Mrs. Barth would think that Al was a barbarian and leave both the dinner table and the agency. Instead, she burst out laughing. Joke after joke, each one dirtier than the one before, and this grandmotherly lady was laughing her head off. From that point on, the relationship was great and the account stayed with Eicoff for years.

SELLING HARD WHEN EVERYONE ELSE SOLD SOFT

In those early years, the Golden Age of Advertising was dawning. Big agencies like Leo Burnett, J. Walter Thompson, Ogilvy & Mather and Foote Cone & Belding were creating 30-second commercials that were funny, dramatic and emotional. Boutique agencies headed by Mary Lawrence, George Lois and Jerry Della Femina were creating edgy, groundbreaking spots. Rating points became the sine qua non for agencies, and reach and frequency were two words in every media buyer's vocabulary.

Al went in the opposite direction, both in terms of creative and media. He created the Theory of Sales Resistance and the Isolation Factor that ran counter to the conventional wisdom. The former held that people watch television either to be entertained or because they're bored, meaning that running a commercial during a highly-rated show was foolish—no one would leave that show during the commercial break to call the number and order the product. On the other hand, if they were watching a rerun, they were probably bored and wouldn't have a problem picking up the phone and ordering.

The isolation factor proposed that if you ran a longer commercial of 90 or 120 seconds, you could dominate a commercial break and isolate the viewer—you wouldn't have to compete with three other 30-second spots.

Similarly, Al mastered the art of the hard sell commercial. He didn't think humor had any place in advertising, and he hated wasting precious seconds on "arty" production that could be better used to make the selling argument. He believed in using hyperbole, in testimonials, in memorable demonstrations of how the product worked.

Al knew how to sell hard and effectively, and he put this talent to use not only in commercials but in his dealings with media representatives.

At most large agencies, television sales reps were treated like second class citizens. In many cases, they had to wait for long periods of time in lobbies until media buyers finished more important tasks. These big agency media buyers often spoke to reps like order takers rather than as partners in a shared enterprise.

Al recognized from the beginning that treating reps fairly and warmly would pay dividends. At A. Eicoff & Co., reps rarely waited in the lobby for long. In many instances, Al would escort them back to his office, telling them dirty jokes on the journey. He'd take them out to lunch and dinner as well as spring for drinks.

And he'd give them his irresistible pitch for lower rates: "Look, you and me, we're on the same side of the desk. So don't think you're just selling me time. The way we work is, the more sales we produce on your shows, the more advertising we give you. So give me the lowest possible rate you can, and if a spot doesn't work at that rate, give me an even lower rate."

More often than not, the reps bought his pitch and gave him what he asked for.

Al also pioneered the concept of a "cash library". Essentially, what it boiled down to was that at times, stations had slots they could fill with commercials, and if they didn't fill them, they could never recover that lost revenue. Al proposed that the stations let him send them tapes of spots, they run them for free, and the agency would pay them a percentage of every order generated. For the stations, it was like found money.

During these years, Al and the agency never gained the respect of the ad community despite his innovations and success. But Al didn't care—the agency was making a lot of money and growing. In fact, he reveled in his role as the black sheep of the advertising family. The media took notice and began writing stories about the man they called "the king of the late night pitchmen".

It was a title Al was ambiguous about at best. While some commercials did run during the wee hours of the night, others did not, and he thought the moniker carried negative connotations. At the same time, Al loved publicity, so if the title got him more stories in newspapers and magazines, he was willing to live with it.

Chapter 2—PIONEERING IN ADVERTISING AND THE CANADIAN WILDERNESS

From 1978 to 1981, Al was often an absentee landlord. Though still the head of the agency, he was more involved in his outside interests—golf, his home in Florida, various investments—than in the agency's operations. When he was involved, it was usually with one of the few remaining clients with gadget-like products; they reminded him of the old days. On more than one occasion, Al and I argued about the agency's clients. Al wanted more Hair Wiz-like clients, but I kept telling him that we needed accounts like Time-Life and Playboy that were sustainable and prestigious. He was never comfortable with those accounts.

Still, he liked being the ceremonial face of the agency—and what a face it was, with that gravelly smoker's voice coming out of it. He rumbled down the agency hallways like a colorful locomotive, his loud plaid jackets contrasting with his blindingly bright pants (not to mention his perpetually stained ties). He'd stick his head in people's offices to tell a joke or question a bill.   He could be impetuous and unpredictable, but he could also inspire loyalty and trust.

The business was doing well, buoyed by accounts such Nu Finish, Roll-O-Matic Mop and Linen Curlers.   It was a transition period, in that while we were adding solid, long-term clients with legitimate products, we still attracted the occasional oddball. Every so often, an inventor or disreputable marketer would enter the agency, convinced that Al Eicoff could put his advertising magic to work for them. Word had spread about the agency's specialized expertise in television advertising, and newspapers and magazines did stories about Al, knowing good copy when they saw it. Al declared the account executive was dead in one column and in another blasted commercials that used humor to sell (Al liked a good joke more than most but didn't believe being funny translated into sales).

Though Al gloried in the publicity and the accounts and profits that flowed from it, he didn't like being portrayed as some sort of advertising flim flam man.

What was true, though, was that Al was brilliant at knowing products that would succeed using television advertising and the ones that wouldn't. I remember a guy visited us with a shoe shine spray-on product. It was demonstrable, offered a clear product benefit and the pricing was right. But when the guy who owned the company said that it would save a user 15 seconds a day (versus shining shoes the old-fashioned way), Al said it would never work: "15 seconds saved a day isn't enough to motivate someone to buy the product".

Al espoused his favorite advertising theories involving the isolation factor and sales resistance, and he did so with great persuasiveness. The former held that longer-length commercials were able to dominate commercial breaks and thereby "isolate" viewers, commanding their attention in a way that shorter spots all clustered together couldn't. The latter suggested that people were more receptive to advertising when they were watching programs in which they didn't have a serious interest—reruns, old movies and the like—and they were more resistant to programs they love, such as high-rated prime time shows. Combined with his approach to media buying and his key outlet marketing strategy with Manny Gutterman, Al had an arsenal of concepts that he could articulate powerfully.

Those concepts, though, didn't require more than the bargain basement budgets. Al wasn't interested in doing more expensive commercials, ones with more sophisticated creative and better production values. He maintained that clients weren't interested in great-looking spots, just how well they sold. I argued that we needed better-looking creative to attract better clients— ones that would bill more and be with us for the long-term. Al was not convinced, and it was another topic about which we battled frequently.

Still, he didn't prevent me from pursuing those higher-level clients, and he recognized that my approach was necessary with many of the prospective clients that walked through the door. Whenever we had a prospective client coming to the agency, Al would appear in my office and ask, "Can you join us?" I loved the interplay between Al and myself in those early years. He would deliver his standard pitch, and I would tailor it to a particular company's needs and objectives. Al had trained me well in the Eicoff way of doing advertising, and he told me time and again that an advertiser has to trust you before they'll hire you. I learned how to build that trust with a wide range of businesses—a range that was often outside of Al's comfort zone.

AN ERA OF CRAZINESS AND FUN

Life with Al at the agency was unpredictable; you never knew what he might do or in front of whom he might do it. Almost every day produced an incident that would generate a lawsuit or protest today, but back then was accepted as part of the nuttiness of the business. Here are just two of the many incidents that Al precipitated:

•The more Al distanced himself from a lot the agency's accounts, the more bored he became when he was in our offices. To relieve the boredom, he would sometime wander around the agency looking for things to fix. One of those things was the Xerox machine located just outside of the conference room. The machine often went on the fritz, and Al liked nothing better than to roll up his sleeves and dig into its innards in an attempt to fix it. One day I brought a new business prospect to the agency, and we were meeting in the conference room. When we took a break for lunch and walked out of the conference room, the prospect said, "I'd like to meet Mr. Eicoff, I've heard a lot about him." At just that moment, we were walking by the Xerox machine, and a guy was on his hands and knees, his clothes stained with printing ink, trying to make the copier work. The portly Xerox machine repairman was wearing a toupee and was wearing a sport coat and a tie. As we approached, the repairman heard the client's request, looked up quizzically, and as we drew up next to him I said, "Mr. Eicoff's not in today," and kept walking past Al, who returned to his Xerox machine repair.

•We were having lunch with a prospective client at a restaurant in the Marriott Hotel and when the check came, Al pulled out a ballpoint pen and signed the credit card slip. He then took the pen and began writing all over the white shirt he was wearing. I thought he had gone mad. Imagine, you're with a client, you've just finished a business lunch in a nice restaurant and the head of the ad agency begins scribbling furiously on his shirt with an ink pen. "What are you doing?" I asked Al, hoping that he might be able to respond rationally. "You'll see," he said in that gruff, know-it-all tone. The client looked at him like he was nuts. We went back to the office, Al pulled out a product from a cabinet in his office and said, "You guys aren't going to believe what you're about to see." The product was a stain remover, and he began dousing his shirt liberally with the product, spritzing himself like a madman. Instead of removing the ink stains, though, the product spread them—his shirt became one massive, widening stain, turning his white shirt blue. Al was shaking his head, muttering, "I don't understand this." I grabbed the product and started reading the label, and at the end of its long list of its applications, there was the line, "Works on everything but ink."

My favorite Al Eicoff story from this period took place around 1976. He showed up at the office one day and asked me what I was doing for lunch. He told me that someone had ripped off the hood ornament on his Rolls Royce and he needed to replace it. I went with him to the Rolls Royce dealer who immediately recognized Al. As we entered, he had a look on his face that I had seen on the faces of others Al had dealt with—a look communicating they wished they were somewhere else. Still, he came up to us and said, "Hello, Mr. Eicoff, what can I do for you?" Al explained that he needed a hood ornament replacement, and the dealer said that it will cost $2000.

"Are you crazy!" Al was livid. "How much for a used one?"

"$500."

Al was outraged, and he looked at me and said, "You know what we're going to do? We're going to a trophy store. I'm going to buy a trophy, glue it on to the hood and no one will know the difference."

The dealer thought Al was kidding, but I knew that he was serious. We drove to a trophy store on

Irving Park Road, went inside and Al found a bowling trophy. He told the clerk he would take it, but to remove the top of it for use as an ersatz Rolls hood ornament. We then drove to Walgreens to purchase Super Glue, and in the parking lot, Al glued the ornament to the car. We then got on Lake Shore Drive heading back downtown, and Al was bursting with pride. "No one can tell it's a bowling trophy!"

The next morning, Al came into my office with his head bowed.

"What's the matter?"

"I was driving on the Dan Ryan and the trophy flew off and smashed my front window. It's going to cost thousands of dollars to fix."

It's worth noting that Al loved when I told this story. In a way, it captured a lot of who he was. He was innovative—replacing a Rolls Royce hood ornament with a bowling trophy. He was willing to take a risk—it didn't pay off, but that's another issue. He was cheap—he could have afforded ten hood ornaments but refused to pay the money out of principle. He was a bit crazy—how many other ad agency CEOs can you imagine affixing a bowling trophy to their Rolls in the parking lot?

AN ECCENTRIC GENIUS

Reading these stories, you might think that Al was kind of crazy. You wouldn't be wrong. But he was also crazy-smart. He was like a mad scientist, experimenting constantly, willing to test 9 approaches that everyone thinks is nuts in order to reach the 10th which becomes a breakthrough.

During this time, Al was making a lot of money from Tarn-X, CLR and Jelmar, purchased a television station in Reno and bought a home in Palm Springs (though he quickly departed from California for a better house in Florida). He had cronies like Manny Gutterman, Marty Himmel (Doan's backache pills, Lavoris mouthwash) and Bernie Mitchell (founder of Jovan, the perfume company) who steered business to the agency and also played golf and caroused with Al. Though Al was spending less and less time at the agency and more and more time on the golf course, he still was the face of the agency and could still work wonders with a certain type of client. But not often and not with many clients. Though he was focused on the agency's bottom line, he usually wasn't involved externally (clients) or internally (agency policies and employees). As long as the bottom line was good and the agency was growing, he didn't care about the agency's dysfunctional aspects.

Al's management style was unusual, to say the least. He was always concerned about the agency's reputation, and that's one of the reasons that he insisted we pay all vendors quickly and in full. At the same time, he had a laissez faire attitude toward what went on in the agency, especially regarding sex and gambling—both were fine by him, as long as it caused no problems with the outside world. An infamous agency party in the '70s was marked by widespread drunkenness and orgy-like behavior.

Al also could be puritanical in certain respects. One day a media buyer came to the office wearing hot pants. Al decided her attire violated his idea of a professional dress code, and he called her into his office saying, "You've got to take those off."

She did so right in front of him.

"Put them back on," he said.

He liked to provoke people with his words and made you think he was capable of anything, but he adhered to his own code of conduct—a code that sometimes was difficult to understand.

Around this time, we discovered that Canada was fertile ground for some of our products. We found two guys who could handle distribution for our clients' products in western and eastern Canada—Bob King was in the west (Ontario) and Jacques Gatien was in the east (Quebec). The first one was Eternalash, a hot product in the U.S. (long-lasting fake eyelashes). I went with the Eternalash client and met with Bob King of Ontario West and made a deal with him—he'd distribute our clients' products and we would buy the television time. Bob suggested we meet with Jacques Gatien, who could do the same type of distribution in Quebec province as well as the eastern provinces.

Then Bob King was arrested and went to jail for bigamy.

We were left holding the bag for $400,000 owed to Canadian television stations. Most agencies would have bankrupted their Canadian operation—we had set it up as a separate legal entity from our U.S. operation to protect us from situations like this. Al, though, refused to walk away from the debt through a bankruptcy strategy. He believed that the agency's reputation was even more important than short-term profit and lost; that to build a sustainable enterprise, you needed a sustainable reputation.

We flew to Canada and met with Jacques and a bunch of attorneys. Sitting in a semi-circle, we're having a very serious discussion about Jacques taking over all of Canada distribution and how we'll pay off the amount owed Canadian stations. Back then, Al was still smoking cigarettes, and as he's talking, he tries to light his cigarette. But instead of pulling out a lighter, he extracted a small canister of Binaca breath spray, and he managed to shoot the spray directly into his eye. Al's head jerked back, the unlit cigarette dangling from his lips, his eye no doubt burning, but he kept talking as if he hadn't just injected chemicals into his eyeball. When it came to money, nothing got in the way of Al's train of thought.

Another time, Al was on the cusp of making a major mistake, leading to the biggest fight Al and I ever had. TV Magic Cards was one of our major accounts, and we had a distribution deal in which we received our standard 15% commission on the advertising, and the distributor received 10% of all product sales for their distribution efforts. That was a fair deal all around.

Nonetheless, one day Al and I met with the distributor, and he told us that TV Magic Cards asked him to reduce his commission. He proposed instead that we reduce our commission.

"You want us to reduce our commission?" I asked, not believing the words coming out of his mouth. "You not only make more money from the account than we do, but we brought you the account!"

The argument escalated. Finally, I'd had enough. Al had watched this unfold without saying anything. I turned to Al and said, "If you agree to this, I won't work for you for one minute longer." I walked out of the office.

As I made my way back to the agency, I thought to myself, "What did you just do?"

When Al returned, he entered my office and said, "You were right. I didn't do it."

O CANADA

Canada became an increasingly important market for the agency, and so when Jacques invited Al, myself and our wives to go fishing on an island he owned in the Canadian wilderness, we went. It sounded as if we would be staying in a luxurious lodge and eat gourmet food and drink fine wine throughout the four-day trip.

They flew us in on sea planes, and when we landed, Al and I brought the luggage to the lodge ahead of our wives. It turned out the lodge was a three-bedroom cabin with plywood walls, mice and dust. It had one toilet for all of us and no phone service. Al was clearly worried, saying, "There's no way Helene (Al's wife) will stay here." But before he could put her back on the plane, it took off, stranding us in the wilderness. Besides Jacques and his wife, there were two other

French women who smoked pot constantly and were wearing evening gowns, the only clothes they had brought with them (apparently, they somehow were under the impression that this trip was going to be to Las Vegas).

The first night, Al, Helene, Linda and I all shared one room and slept in the same bed. In the middle of the night, I woke up suddenly, certain that a train was roaring through the center of the cabin. I searched about wildly for the source of the sound and located it: Al was snoring so loudly that the room seemed to be vibrating. I shook him and told him to stop, and he did...for a few minutes. Then he began snorting and snuffling again, even louder than before if that was possible. I poked and prodded him, he stopped for a few minutes, then resumed his noise-making. This went on the entire night.

The next morning, Al and I woke early to go fishing—this was Al's plan, and he was excited. I explained to Al that I had never fished before, but shortly after throwing the line in the water, I caught a small fish. Al was genuinely excited; he acted like it was the greatest fish ever caught. He was proud of me in the same way that he was when I brought in an account.

Aside from this fishing experience, though, the claustrophobia and discomfort of the cabin was getting to Al and I and our wives. We had sufficient food and wine in the cabin for four days. On the fifth day when a plane was supposed to fly in and pick us up, a dense fog descended and it couldn't land. Linda and I slept in the living room after that first night, preferring the mice there to Al's snoring—at least the mice were quiet.

I figured if we could survive all that, dealing with Al's craziness in the familiar world of business would be a piece of cake.

Chapter 3—THE TRANSITION TO OGILVY

No one but Alvin Eicoff could turn a heart attack into a slapstick comedy routine.

In the Spring of 1979, Al and Jerry Siegel took a break from work to play racquetball. Al should have known better. He smoked constantly, was overweight and a Type A personality vulnerable to heart problems. Anyone else would have declined Jerry's invitation to play, but Al was so intensely competitive, he couldn't resist the opportunity to beat Jerry.

In the middle of the game, Al collapsed and was rushed to Northwestern Hospital. It was touch and go, and the doctors weren't sure if he would survive as they worked on him in the Intensive Care Unit. Fortunately, Al pulled through and word spread quickly about his brush with death.

When he was out of danger and in recovery, we began informing friends and colleagues about his heart attack. I knew there was one more person Al would want us to get in touch with: his mistress, Marilyn. Jerry and I flipped a coin to see who would make that call and Jerry lost. He informed her of what was taking place and said that under no circumstances should she visit since Helene, Al's wife, was there.

Al was conscious but drugged up and attached to various devices as he recovered in the ICU. One day, Jerry and Jules Lenard from our New York office stopped by the ICU to see how Al was doing, and his wife Helene was also there. They talked quietly, worried about Al and how his health problems would affect him personally as well as the agency. Jerry's attention was caught by something just outside the room. He saw someone hovering in the corridor and couldn't believe what he was seeing.

A white-uniformed hospital cleaning lady armed with a mop stood there; she wanted to come in Al's room and clean up. Not a big deal, right? Except it wasn't a cleaning lady; it was Marilyn dressed up as one. Al's mistress was as headstrong as he was and apparently unperturbed that Al's wife was in the same room.

She sauntered in, and as she did, Al looked up and saw who the visitor was. Suddenly, the blood pressure monitor began flashing and emitting high-pitched warning beeps. Other monitors erupted—it was a miracle that the sight of Marilyn and Helene in the same room didn't kill Al on the spot. Nurses and doctors rushed in, and the look on Al's face was one of pure terror—he was terrified of the confrontation between the two women. Fortunately, Jerry took Helene by the elbow and escorted her out of the room. "We have to let the doctors do their work, and besides, I have an important matter to discuss with you." She went grudgingly, and when she tried to return to the room, Jerry said, "I think it will be better for Al if you stay out here."

Truer words were never spoken.

Despite the shock of seeing his mistress in the same room with his wife, Al recovered. After being released from the hospital, he went to California to recuperate and lose weight.

As Al convalesced, Jules Lenard and Jerry Siegel plotted. They were like the members of the royal court who believed the king had abdicated his throne. Given this belief, they planned a coup.

I received a call on a Sunday night from Marty Grossman, who operated our New York office with Jules. He warned me that Jerry and Jules were going to capitalize on Al's absence and try to seize control of the agency. I wasn't particularly worried for a number of reasons, including my knowledge that Al had placed a legal document in a safe stating that if anything happened to him, I was to take over the agency.

As soon as I walked into the office on Monday, Jerry and Jules entered my office and told me that "We're having a meeting of the agency to discuss accounts."

"Good," I said. "Feel free to discuss your accounts, but I'm not going to attend." As they knew, they barely had three accounts between them. I'm not sure how or why they thought they might seize control of the agency, but their coup ended before it began.

Nonetheless, the agency's direction was uncertain until Al returned shortly after Xmas. Employees were anxious about what might happen next, especially because Al had been a disinterested and often absent CEO before his health problems. If anything, his return to the office created even greater anxiety—no one was certain what Al was going to do.

About a month after Al's return, he asked me to come to his office, and sitting there were Dave Marguiles and Jerry Pickholtz from Ogilvy in New York. That was when I learned that Al was contemplating selling the agency. In February, Ogilvy asked that I come to New York and meet with their leadership team. After meeting them, it quickly became apparent that this would be a golden opportunity for me.

"How did it go?" Al asked when I returned from two days of meetings.

"I love them," I said. "This is going to be the best thing that ever happened to me. But it will be the worst thing that ever happened to you."

"What do you mean?" Al barked, growing defensive.

"They're not your type of people. You'll hate it."

"Nah, they'll figure out how smart I am and make me chairman of the board, you'll see."

I told him I didn't think that would be the case, but Al being Al, he wasn't listening; he was absolutely convinced that their leadership team would view him the way they viewed David Ogilvy. For someone who was so smart and perceptive about some things, he could be dense about others.

For a month or two, nothing happened. Then Al called me into his office and closed the door.

"You're the president," he said.

"What do you mean?"

"What do you think it means?"

"Why are you doing this now?

"Ogilvy wants management in place before they buy the agency."

Before finalizing the deal, David Ogilvy flew to Chicago to meet with me and Al. For me, it was like meeting Babe Ruth. For anyone in advertising at that time, David was a hero. During our lunch with David, Al was uncharacteristically reserved. Perhaps unconsciously, Al knew that it was a flawed deal from the start. But Al being Al, he was not about to turn down the money they were offering. Specifically, Al would receive $4 million for the sale. But the flaw was that the agency only made $100,000 that year, far below what Al's projections were. Ogilvy made a deal with Al that they would pay him $2 million initially and the additional $2 million would come out of the agency's profits over the following years. This meant that every penny the agency spent came out of Al's pocket. It was a bad deal, since it motivated Al to spend as little money as possible—a policy that ended up driving a wedge between Al and me.

But I'm getting ahead of myself. At the moment of the meeting with David Ogilvy, all I knew was that Al and the Ogilvy philosophy didn't mix. Their philosophy was that creative helps attract clients, and they believed strongly in advertising that had high production values and projected a strong image for the brand. Al, on the other hand, believed that creative was a vehicle for clients to spend money. I knew that as part of Ogilvy, we had to improve our creative to attract clients—both theirs and ours. Al didn't agree with this idea.

For this reason, I warned him about what this deal would mean, that he would feel like a fish out of water. It wasn't just a philosophical clash with Ogilvy, but a cultural one as well. But he couldn't see it. He didn't perceive that his rough, colorful and eccentric ways were a poor match for the Ogilvy culture, which prized civility and protocol. The Jewish kid from Montana with the loud sports jackets and food-stained ties and off-color jokes was ill-suited to Ogilvy.

Still, nothing happened during the next few months, and I wondered if it might fall through. I was approached by Hank Feely, the international president of Leo Burnett, and he took us out of dinner and wondered if we had ever considered selling the agency. So we had another suitor. Part of me selfishly hoped that Ogilvy would buy us, knowing that it would be great for my career. Part me was protective of Al and worried that if it happened, he would be hurt.

I was on a business trip in the Cincinnati airport when I picked up a newspaper and saw the headline: OGILVY AND EICOFF TO MERGE.

And then the trouble began. Ogilvy, upon realizing that Al's projection of $1 million in revenue was actually $100,000, told him that they couldn't pay him $4 million but would pay him $2 million, but that he wouldn't receive that sum until revenue reached a certain point. That meant that every dollar the agency spent came out of Al's pocket, delaying his payout.

As a result, Al, who was frugal by nature, became Ebenezer Scrooge. He told me not to spend any money, since it was _his_ money I was spending. When I promoted someone to head one of our departments, I gave this individual a raise and Al went crazy. I told Al that I had all the responsibility and he had all the financial authority, and that wasn't working.

Our relationship deteriorated, and the agency was in shambles. We had a creative director who was an alcoholic, the computer system didn't work and everyone was worried if the agency's culture would change when it was officially part of Ogilvy.

In this environment, I needed Al's support, but what I often received was his opposition. Alex was the head of our Canadian business, and shortly after Al named me president, Alex asked me to take an action that I thought was a bad idea, so I told him no. Shortly thereafter, Al appears in my office and sits across from me and begins rocking back and forth like an autistic child. I know that this behavioral tic was a sign that Al felt like he was on uncertain ground.

"Alex came to me and told me you said no, but I think you should do what he's asking."

I rose from my chair, looked him directly in the eye and said, "I think you should be president of the agency," and walked out. He caught up to me and said, "Okay, okay, come back, I won't do that again."

But of course, he did it again and again. I don't think he could help himself. Somewhere in the back of his mind, he must have known that selling the agency was a mistake for him. But he couldn't admit it, so he tried to sabotage me. I knew he didn't view it that way, but Al was complicated and a little crazy, so it would take a trained psychologist to figure out what was going on in his head. All I knew was that he was making this transitional period more difficult than it had to be.

After the sale became reality, though, I was excited. They flew me to Monaco for an Ogilvy worldwide conference, I met the heads of offices from around the world, walked around with David Ogilvy and was tremendously impressed by their people and their vision. When I returned to the office and told Al about the trip, he bowed his head and looked sad.

"What's the matter?" I asked him.

"You don't love me anymore." He said it like a father to his son.

"What do you mean?"

"You love Ogilvy."

"Can't a child love two parents?"

Apparently not, since Al left the office without another word.

Things were getting out of control. Al was firing off memos to CEO Bill Phillips at Ogilvy, suggesting all sorts of crazy ideas for Ogilvy to implement: he wanted them to stop doing all their research as well as create their own channel to slow client commercials. I had become friends with Bill, and he called, asking what could he do to get Al to stop bothering him.

"How about sending him around the world on a speaking trip in which he can educate people about Direct Response Television Advertising?"

Bill loved the idea, and so did Al. The first stop on his lecture tour was the Ogilvy office in the Philippines. They held a cocktail party for all their clients and spouses, the type of affair where the dress is formal and people are on their best behavior. On top of that, this is a society where good manners are prized and customs are observed. Now imagine Al with his loud, grating voice, louder and more grating attire and his obliviousness to the cultural issues. For whatever reason, Al determined that it would be a good idea to do magic tricks, and he managed to offend the wife of the Philippines agency's biggest client with his act.

"We're recalling Al," Bill said shortly after he heard about the incident.

When Al returned, he came up to me and said, "They've recalled me."

"Why?" I asked.

"I have no idea."

And perhaps he really didn't. Al created his own reality, and in that reality, he was guilty of nothing more than an "innocent" party trick.

Things got worse. Al riled up Ogilvy in a number of different ways. He'd just had his book, OR YOUR MONEY BACK, published, and he created a direct response television commercial to help sell it. In the commercial, Al pitched the book by saying, "What David Ogilvy paid millions for, you can learn for the price of this book." I showed the commercial to Ogilvy's leadership team, and they were understandably aghast—Al was essentially telling millions of viewers (not to mention clients) that David Ogilvy was a sucker for paying so much for the agency when everyone else could get the same knowledge by paying $20 for the book. Bill Phillips asked me how a DRTV commercial like this worked.

"He'll test the spot, and as long as it's profitable, it will continue to run."

"Call me if it's profitable," Bill said.

It wasn't, fortunately, and another crisis passed.

But the big crisis was just around the corner.

Al started writing notes to Bill about how he thought I was making bad decisions. In reality, the agency was doing great, and we were flourishing in large

60

part because we were getting a lot of new business from Ogilvy clients.

But that didn't matter to Al, and our relationship deteriorated further. Then, right before our annual Xmas party, he announced over the loudspeaker that all officers of the agency should come to his office. We gathered there, and Al asked us to close the door.

"There's good news, and there's bad news," he said. "The bad news is there are no bonuses or profit sharing this year."

"What's the good news?" I asked, hoping for something, anything, that might stop everyone in the room from starting a job search.

"The good news is that you all still have jobs, now get out of here."

It was unconscionable. Not only didn't the financial performance of the agency justify his actions, but to do it right before the agency Xmas party was the sort of thing only a stereotypical movie villain would do.

I called Bill Phillips the next day, described Al's good news/bad news decree and said that if he didn't remove Al, he'd lose everyone else.

When Al learned I had called Bill and what our conversation had been about, he called in a white-hot rage: "Why did you do that? You turned on me!"

"You didn't give me a choice," I said, hanging up.

Shortly thereafter, both Al and I were summoned to New York. Though we flew together, we didn't exchange a word. We arrived at Bill Phillips office, and Dave Margulies was also in the room. I had no idea what would happen next, and I was prepared to resign rather than endure one more day of an intolerable situation.

Bill started the meeting by handing Al a check for $2 million. "You are no longer involved with the agency financially. You can remain in the office, but you no longer have any say in agency matters. And Ron, Dave will be joining the agency to deal with all the financial issues."

Al accepted the check and put it into his pocket.

As we walked out of the building, Al asked me if I wanted to have lunch. I said sure, glad that Al seemed to have accepted his removal, comforted no doubt by the

$2 million check. We went to a nearby place and Al ordered a turkey sandwich.

"And can I have some extra mayo?" he asked the waitress.

"Sure, but that will be an additional 25 cents."

"Forget it," Al said.

This was Alvin. He had just received two million dollars, but he refused to spend 25 cents for the mayonnaise he wanted. He was a walking, talking contradiction. I believed he loved me like a son. But at the same time, he was jealous of my success and had trouble accepting that it was me and not him leading the agency.

Two or so years after we joined Ogilvy, we decided to move across the street to our current location. Our old offices at 525 N. Michigan were no longer adequate for our growing agency—it wasn't in great condition, and the occasional cockroach emerged, not the best impression to make on clients. When I told Al I had decided to move the agency, he said, "I'm not moving. You didn't consult me, and I like it here."

I tried to convince him to move with us. Despite our battles, it was inconceivable to me that he would cease to be a physical presence at the agency. I teared up, almost begging him to reconsider.

"Okay," he said. "I'll move on one condition."

Uh oh, I thought. Was he going to ask for an office twice as big as mine? A sizable cash bonus for doing what I requested?

"My condition is that I want an all-white office."

And that's what he got. It looked ridiculous— like a semi-classy hair salon—but it somehow suited him. He was in Florida when we made the move, but when he returned, I greeted him in his blindingly white office and said, "Now it feels like Eicoff."

Chapter 4—A LEGENDARY FIGURE

After the sale of the agency and the move to our new headquarters at 401 N. Michigan Avenue, Al and I still had our tense moments, but they were fewer and less intense than in the past. Part of reason for this was that after the agency sale and the resolution of his financial issues with Ogilvy, he lacked the motivation to challenge my decisions. In fact, when he showed up at the agency, he often acted like he never sold it—he rarely talked about anything to do with Ogilvy. Because he didn't have to deal with them, he could pretend like they didn't exist.

But the main reason our relationship improved was that I helped get him into the Direct Marketing Association (DMA) Hall of Fame.

THE BLACK SHEEP TAKEN INTO THE FOLD

For years, we had tried and failed to convince the DMA to admit Al to the Hall of Fame. At the time, it was a heavily print-focused organization, and television direct response was seen as a competitive threat, siphoning off ad dollars from direct mail. Perhaps even more significantly, Al had never made an effort to curry favor with anyone in the DMA. No doubt, he had offended some members, either because of his manner or his evangelical advocacy of television.

Given DRTV's prominence today, it may be hard to imagine a time when it was seen as the black sheep. But it wasn't that long ago when I witnessed the bias against it first hand. The DMA was holding its annual conference in Chicago, and they had just named a new President—let's call him Bob. At the conference, one of my colleagues and I introduced ourselves to him, and we started talking about how the DMA didn't welcome agencies like ours and seemed to wish we weren't members. Bob nodded and said, "We didn't want your ilk in our organization."

It was like the head of an exclusive country club telling me that "We don't want your kind here." Later, after I calmed down, I wrote a letter to Bob making the case for DRTV, and I think he softened his stance. Still, he never spoke up for Al and his inclusion in the Hall of Fame.

I was able to get on the Hall of Fame nominating committee, and in my first year on the committee, Al didn't receive a single vote. The following year, I gathered endorsement letters from Ted Turner and other luminaries lauding Al for his innovations and accomplishments. I sent these letters to everyone on the committee. On the first round of voting, Al received three votes.

I was incensed. I lectured my fellow members about how for years the DMA had treated DRTV like a step child rather than a member of the family. Worth Linden, who had worked at Wunderman and knew how much Al had contributed to our business, reinforced my message, insisting that the committee members look at the endorsement letters again. Worth asked, "How could you not vote him in?"

This time, he received the necessary votes and was accepted in the Hall of Fame.

From that point on, Al's attitude toward me changed. Al may not have been one for awards, but inclusion in the Hall of Fame was immensely meaningful for him. He saw that even though we disagreed about many things, I was his champion, not his adversary. Afterwards, he wrote me the following letter:

Please accept this gift as a small token for your years of loyalty, helpfulness and friendship. I say a "small token" because nothing can repay you for the time and effort you put in for so many causes on my behalf.

If I had a biological son, I would only hope he would turn out like you. I've always treasured my relationship with you, Linda, Debbie and Michael.

Al

The gift alluded to in the letter was a clock that displayed the time from locations all over the world. The clock never worked well, and I assume that Al must have gotten a deal on it, but his heart was in the right place.

THE AGENCY GROWS BUT AL WAS NOT
ALWAYS A GROWN UP

Al became a more benign and infrequent
presence after we moved to 401 N. Michigan Avenue.
Typically, he was in the office during the summer, but
his main focus was on CLR and TarnX because of his
ownership stake in those Eicoff clients. I still tried to
involve Al by having him speak to the agency at a series
of luncheons, but aside from these infrequent talks, he
was often absent.

Despite Al's decreased involvement, every so
often we called upon him when it seemed he was well-
suited to meet with a particular client. Around 1990 we
were contacted by a Las Vegas casino who thought we
might be the right agency to help them market
themselves, and a young account supervisor, Bill
McCabe (now Eicoff's CEO) was invited to visited their
headquarters. I don't recall exactly how Al became
involved, but if anyone at the agency seemed at home in
Vegas, it was Al. He and Bill traveled there to meet
with Bob Stupak.

Al may have been the last of the crazies, but at the time, other crazies still ran companies, and Bob was one of them. Besides owning the Vegas World casino, Bob was known as a world-class poker player, having won the World Series of Poker as well as a $1 million bet on the Super Bowl. He also donated $100,000 to the United Negro College Fund in exchange for a chance to play with the Harlem Globetrotters. And he once paid a guy $1 million to jump off the top of Vegas World (presumably with a parachute or into a net) and then charged him a $990,000 "landing fee".

Al and Bill arrive at the casino and meet with one of Bob's assistants, Ira, who had just been released from prison. While they're waiting in Ira's office for Bob, Ira is taking bets—from his 10-year-old and 12-year-old sons. Bob still isn't available, so Ira takes them to the nearby Sands Casino and tells them they should play blackjack. But when they start playing, the pit boss, who has been eyeing Ira, whispers something to the dealer, who after one hand tears up all six decks. He re-deals, then tears up another six decks. It turned out that Ira was a card-counter, and the pit boss had spotted him.

The group moves on to a restaurant to have lunch, and they're joined by Bob's lawyer, who has a shirt open to his navel and a number of thick gold chains hanging from his neck. At this point, Al and Bill are wondering where Bob is. It turns out that he's sitting few feet away at an adjacent table, and he comes over to join them.

They introduced themselves, shake hands, and they notice that Bob is missing two fingers.

Bob stares at Al and says, "I've heard a lot of things about you. How old are you?"

Al tells him his age and Bob says, "I'll bet you $100,000 you aren't that old."

As Bill tells it, this is the first time that he's ever seen Al at a loss for words. Bill looks over at Al and he can almost hear Al's brain whirring as he's trying to figure out what Bob's game is. Al knows his own age, but he figures that he must be missing something.

He declines to take the bet.

Later, Bob says, "You should have taken the bet. I have no idea how old you really are."

It was one of the few times that Al was treated to a taste of his own medicine.

NOT AL'S KIND OF CREATIVE

During this time, we began upgrading our creative department, bringing in key people like Larry Vienna and letting go of others such as Joel Rappin, who was the head of the department. When Joel left, Al kept pressing me as to who I was going to hire—the two creative directors, Larry and Carole Darr, didn't want the position. I told Al we needed someone who could provide a huge creative upgrade—an upgrade that struck Al as unnecessary. I tried to explain to him that we couldn't attract certain types of clients without better creative, but Al was unconvinced.

When I hired Sandy Stern, it provided the creative transformation that we desperately needed. Though Sandy was charming and polite with Al, he was always intimidated by her. He knew how smart and accomplished she was and came from a creative world that wouldn't let him set foot in their territory. The gap between her and Al's approach to creative was chasm-like. For instance, we had started doing a lot of work for Sears and had created image-oriented spots. It was a big client, and we were all focused on doing a great job for them. Al, aware of their importance to the agency, tried to help. He returned from Florida, walked into my office and announced in his most serious voice: "I have the answer for Sears. Come with me, I'm going to tell Sandy what it is, this will change everything Sears does creatively."

We walk into her office, and I explain that Al has come up with an idea to turn around Sears' business.

"Tell us what it is," I said to Al.

"Dwarfs."

"Dwarfs?"

"There are these appliance commercials in Florida, they've got two dwarfs as the presenters, and they're knocking them dead. We have to take this to Sears."

I'll never forget the look on Sandy's face; she couldn't believe that he was serious but suspected that he was.

"Let me digest this for a little while, then I'll get back to you," she said, knowing that his idea was not even remotely viable.

As amusing as Al's ideas could be, they could also be harmful. Remember, Al was a legendary figure to many employees at this point, and when he weighed in on a subject, they paid attention. When he suggested using dwarfs in a Sears spot, we could all laugh at the outrageousness of it. Other times, however, no one was laughing.

We had a healthcare products client, Galderma, that marketed acne treatment products. We had created commercials for them that won awards and helped their sales skyrocket. We had just completed what I thought was our best commercials for them to date, and I was excited to show them to Al. I had prepped him about the spot, explaining how well they were working. I knew that Al valued results above all else.

I gathered the entire creative department in Larry Vienna's office and we showed the commercials. When they were done playing, I turned to Al and asked him what he thought.

"I wouldn't have done them this way," he said and walked out without another word.

It was like a slap in the face. The room was stunned silent.

I stormed out of Larry's office and confronted Al in his office.

"It worked!" I said, barely able to control my rage. "It's all the things we've always talked about. It's not hard-sell, but it sold hard. You and I, we've always talked about how well our advertised products do, and this one is breaking sales records. I just don't understand you."

I didn't talk to Al for the next few days. Finally, he approached me in the hallway and said sheepishly, "The spots really worked?"

"You owe the creative department an apology."

"I'm not apologizing," he said, stubborn to a fault.

I called a meeting of the creative department and explained that Al's perception of creative was different than ours and told them I thought the commercials were great and they represented the direction of the agency.

With hindsight, I think the problem was that Al knew he wasn't capable of creating these types of commercials; the spots that he helped create for TarnX and CLR followed the same creative formula that he had used in the '50s and '60s. When he saw the Galderma spots as well as other work we were doing for Sears and Time-Life, he must have recognized that time was passing him by, and he didn't like it.

BELOVED BUT BEDEVILING

It usually was difficult to stay mad at Al for long. Invariably, he'd do something that was hilarious or helpful and you'd forgive his trespasses. For instance, when Sears was a client, we did a number of spots for them that featured Bob Vila, the celebrity handyman and Sears spokesperson. During the course of our relationship with Sears, Bob got to know Al and was aware that he was the founder of our agency and a legendary figure in the industry.

We were shooting a Sears spot in Miami with Bob, and he came up to me in the hotel lobby with a concerned look on his face.

"Ron, I recently saw something that upset me."

"What is it?" I asked.

"Is Al having problems?"

"What kind of problems?"

"He's kind of down on his luck, having trouble making ends meet?"

Dumbstruck, I asked him why he thought that.

"Well, I was going into a Dunkin Donuts on Chicago's north side early one morning, maybe around 5:30 a.m., and when I went to place my order, the guy behind the counter was Al. I figured things must be tight if he has to work two jobs at his age, especially if he has to get up at the crack of dawn to man the counter at a donut shop."

Rather than address Bob's concern directly, I pointed out the window of the Fontainebleau Hotel where we were staying in Miami. Down in the harbor a huge yacht was moored. Directing Bob's attention toward it, I said, "If Al's struggling, he can always sell his yacht—that's his."

Why was Al working at a Dunkin Donuts at 5:30 a.m.? He had bought a franchise for his son, Jeff, but Jeff was either unable or unwilling to get up at that hour. So Al being Al, he took it upon himself to sell coffee and donuts himself. As the son of a shopkeeper, Al probably didn't see anything unusual about the chairman of an ad agency selling donuts.

In his later years, Al was only an occasional presence in the agency (and not because he spent much time at the donut shop), but he was still capable of making his presence felt. Sometimes, he acted goofy, hiding people's lunches and chortling at his schoolboy stunt. At times, he said and did things that were wildly inappropriate.

We brought the entire agency together to celebrate an executive's 20th anniversary, and I talked about all the contributions this executive had made. I asked Al if he wanted to say a few words.

Al nodded, stood, looked at the executive and said, "Maybe you should get another day job."

He was joking, but it was a completely inappropriate given the occasion. Once again, Al had managed to create an uncomfortable silence during a celebration. Al didn't have a filter; he would say the first thing that came to mind.

I'm sure that at this point, Al was acutely aware of the distance between the agency he founded and the agency that had evolved from his original idea. Despite this distance, Al's influence on how the agency operated and its culture remained. His philosophy of putting the television station reps on the same side of the desk—of treating them like equals and creating a partnership—was precedent-setting and continues to this day.

Al is probably the only agency head who, when a piece of new business came in, never said, "How much will they spend?" He knew that if we could make it work, we would make money and they'd made money, and if it didn't, it would go away. The idea of treating the client's money like it was our own was something in which Al truly believed.

To this day, Al still affects our culture. Eicoff is probably the only major ad agency where people leave at

5:00 and don't work on weekends. His attitude always was that employees are not children; that if they do their jobs well, they should feel free to put in no more than eight hours on weekdays plus have a two-hour lunch if they wanted.

PERSONAL RELATIONSHIPS

Al's relationships with his wife, his mistress, his friends and his kids were different. I'm not judging him on this part of his life, but I know that he struggled with some of these relationships more than most people do—especially his relationships with his sons, Jeff and Larry.

One day Al asked me to come to his office, and after I entered he requested that I close the door and have a seat.

What's this about, I wondered, knowing that the request meant he had something serious to discuss.

"Let me ask your advice. Larry is asking me for money. He wants to buy a plane. Should I give him the money?"

"You really want my advice?"

"Yes," Al said.

"Cut him off."

"What do you mean, cut him off? How will he eat?"

"Have him get a job."

"No, I couldn't ask him to do that."

"Look," I said, "nothing is going to change if you're not going to make him responsible. You dole out money and use it as a control, but you've ruined his life and Jeff's life too. They're beholden to you.

"I can't do that."

"Then don't ask my advice."

Jeffrey, Al's younger son, came into my office one day and said, "Ron, can I borrow $75,000?"

I couldn't imagine why he was asking me for that large sum of money and I asked him what he wanted it for, thinking maybe there was a health emergency.

"I want to buy a horse."

Jeff explained that Larry had bought a horse for $75,000 and sold it for twice as much, and so he wanted to do the same thing, adding that he could make a good living this way.

"Ask your father for the money," I said.

"I did. He won't give it to me."

"Then why do you think I would give to you?"

It was nuts that Jeff was asking this of me, but the apple doesn't fall far from the tree.
I like to think that Al was nuts in both the good and bad senses of that term. I loved when Al dropped by the agency. It was as if everything was aligned by his presence. He had karma, and some of it always rubbed off on the rest of us. Al's name was on the door, and I always tried to remind people of all the pioneering moves he had made. Our lunches together were fewer and fewer as time went on, but I always relished those lunches.

He was one of the last of the crazies. He could create great upheaval and consternation, but he could also create a singular ad agency. And like most crazies, he was never boring and always entertaining.

Chapter 5—ELEVATING THE INDUSTRY

It wasn't just that Al helped create a great ad agency; it was that he made great contributions to advertising in general. I've alluded to some of these contributions previously, but I would be remiss if I didn't tell the business story behind the person. Al understood in his bones how to use advertising to sell. He was a natural.

I'm convinced that one reason his contributions aren't more widely known is his persona. Unlike David Ogilvy and other advertising giants, he didn't sound erudite, give inspiring speeches or develop a network of thought leaders. Instead, as you've probably noticed from the stories I've told, he could be politically incorrect and alienating.

He so offended powerful Chicago Tribune marketing columnist George Lazarus that the journalist refused to accept Al's calls. Unlike other agency heads, Al didn't curry favor with anyone. He was always his authentic self, and his behavior rubbed some people the wrong way.

Al really was a visionary; he just didn't look like one.

Think about some of his contributions.

He was one of the first to recognize that ratings points weren't the only way to buy media; that more-cost effective methods existed.

Al pioneered the use of longer-length commercials. As someone who grasped sales as well or even better than he grasped advertising, he recognized the value of time; that you were more likely to make a sale if you had one or two minutes to make your pitch rather than a paltry 30 seconds.

And Alvin was brilliant at doing something that challenges even the best advertising minds: convincing viewers to get off their couches and respond to the offer. Using demonstrations, testimonials and other tactics, Al was a direct response pioneer. He was in touch with his audiences, and he grasped what would motivate them to dial a number and order a product.

Earlier, I noted that Al was a visionary, and by that I meant that he foresaw where technology was heading as early as the late '70s. At the time, Warner

Cable was developing a system called Qube that introduced people to interactive television. Subscribers to the service received pay-per-view movie channels and a wide variety of other programming. Though Qube ultimately failed, Al saw how with improved technology, this was the future. He was aware all those years ago that viewers wanted choices, and that if cable provided them, television advertising could not only be a mass medium but a targeted strategy to reach niche audiences.

Al was gone before the term, "analytics", became part of the marketing lexicon, but he recognized the value of the concept from the moment he opened the agency's doors for business. Unlike many advertising professionals at the time, Al was intensely interested in how a commercial "performed". For that reason, he always tested spots. He always wanted to know what stations, times and shows delivered the best results. He recognized the value of testing a one-minute spot versus a two-minute commercial and determining which produced the most sales.

Al disdained awareness scores and awards as measures of a commercial's worth. He wanted to know the numbers. In this way, he could analyze what combination of factors would serve the client best.

And speaking of clients, Al connected with them, especially when in the early years when he was fully engaged with the agency. They appreciated his innate ability to sell, and he appreciated their products that were well-suited to his sales-oriented television advertising approach. More than that, though, they saw in Alvin a kindred spirit. Unlike many of the slick ad agency people in the '60s and '70s, Al was genuine. Clients saw that he really cared about their advertising objectives, and he translated that caring into commercials that met and exceeded their goals.

During my career, I learned a lot from Al, and I believe there's still a lot everyone can learn from him. Yes, he made mistakes, and yes, he didn't always adapt well to a changing industry, but he was an original with original ideas. These ideas are the foundation of the agency's success, and perhaps even more significantly, they have migrated into creative, media buying and even digital strategies throughout the business.

Chapter 6—THE SEVENTH STORY

As the last chapter, this is a difficult one for me to write. I've genuinely enjoyed revisiting my journey with Al by telling the stories that illustrate who he was and my relationship with him. Now, though, I have the same feeling as I had when I delivered the eulogy at his funeral—a sense of finality.

At the same time, I want to take advantage of this last opportunity to reflect on who Al was, both as a person and as a professional. In terms of the latter, let me tell you about a trip we took a few months before his death.

I had been invited to speak at the Mid-Florida Advertising Association in Stuart, Florida. Since Stuart was relatively close to Al's Florida apartment and because I wanted to see him, I invited him to join me. I flew in the day before, and then Al and I drove to the talk. The drive was wonderful, since it gave Al and I a chance to reminisce. Al told the stories that he had told a million times before but hearing them for what I knew would be the last time was especially gratifying. Al was in declining health, but he still could muster the energy and the memory to tell the stories we both loved.

We arrived for the talk, and Al was seated on the dais—I had informed the programming committee that Al would be attending and they graciously reserved a prominent spot for him. At the same time, his presence only a few feet away from me was almost surreal. I had given hundreds of speeches during my career, but Al had never been at any of them. It was as if I were a student presenting my paper in front of my favorite professor. I had no idea how he'd respond, especially because I was talking about advertising strategies and showing commercials that wouldn't have existed if not for Al.

After I finished my talk, I opened things up for questions, telling the audience they should feel free to address them to Al as well as myself. A number of good but expected questions were asked, and then came the question I'll never forget. It's important to note that this was 2002, given the following question from a man in the audience: "When do you think the world will be connected through the internet?" Remember, this was a time when global connectivity through social media and various devices was still evolving, and no one really knew what the future would bring.

I told the questioner, "I'm not sure, but it's coming. The world will change."

Then the man asking the question turned to Al and said, "Mr. Eicoff, when do you think this will happen?"

Al looked up, waited a beat and said, "Tuesday."

This one word was the epitome of Al Eicoff: profound, funny, provocative.

Let me share one other story that was neither profound nor provocative, though I think it says something important about the complex person that Al was. I'm reminded of it by the previous story, if only because both took place in Florida. Years earlier, Al had come into my office and announced excitedly that the Home Shopping Network wanted to hire the agency and that one of the top guys there had invited us to their offices in Florida—I don't recall his name, but let's call him Fred. We flew to Tampa, rented a car and showed up at the appointed time at their headquarters.

We walked up to the receptionist and Al said we had an appointment. The receptionist made a call to Fred's secretary and then turned to us and said we weren't on Fred's schedule.

"That's ridiculous," Al said. "We had an appointment, he told us to come down to Florida."

The receptionist made another call and told us that Fred was in a meeting, but that if we could wait a bit, he could squeeze us in for a few minutes.

We're finally escorted into Fred's office, where he greets Al warmly, then asks, "What brings you guys here?"

"You asked us to come down, you said you wanted to hire us."

Fred said he had not called or communicated that intent.

Al thought for a moment, then looked at me and said, "I wonder who called?"

Al's mind didn't work like anyone else's. Instead of being angry or blaming someone, he wondered who called to invite us to Florida. Obviously, no one did. But something must have happened to convince Al that Fred had issued this invitation and wanted to hire the agency. I knew there was no point in questioning him about it, since his thought process was so Byzantine that I would never get a straight answer— and he was probably incapable of supplying one.

The same man who could send us on a wild goose chase to Florida could also say "Tuesday" and sum up the future in a single, thought-provoking word.

I went back to Florida to see Al in January, taking him and Helene out to breakfast. He had trouble just getting out of the car, and his death two months later wasn't a surprise, though it still was a shock to have someone who was so integral to my life for all those years no longer be there.

Shortly after Al's death, his younger son, Jeffrey, came to see me in my office before the funeral. He handed me a sheet of paper, telling me it was his father's eulogy.

"Oh, you wrote it?"

"No," Jeff said, "my dad wrote his own eulogy for the rabbi to read."

"Then why are you showing it to me?"

"I want to get your opinion on whether we should have the rabbi read it."

I started reading and I couldn't believe the words Al had written. No, I told him, this is too embarrassing for everyone. "Don't have him read it."

"Well," Jeff said after thinking about my response, "my father wanted it read."

"Then why did you ask me?"

Anyone who attended Al's funeral will remember it for the rest of his or her life. When the rabbi started reading Al's eulogy, I cringed, knowing what was coming.

"If I wasn't dead, you wouldn't be here today."

That was typical Al, making the most inappropriate joke of his life—or his afterlife. From there it got worse. Much worse.

First, the rabbi read Al's apology to his wife for "numerous marital indiscretions."

Then: "To my sons, you've always disappointed me and never lived up to my expectations. Ron was really the only son I ever had."

As the rabbi read, you could see how uncomfortable he was delivering these words to the hundreds of people in attendance. People shifted in their seats, looked at their shoes or shook their heads in incredulity. Perhaps Al felt that this was his last opportunity to be honest, but his honesty was hurting people who cared most about him.

Then it was my turn. As I walked toward the bimah, I passed Al's casket and said, "Al, you were always a tough act to follow; what did you do to me?"

I told Al Eicoff stories. I had identified seven of them that I thought appropriate, but I only told six of them--all of them are in this book. I couldn't tell the seventh one. Deep inside, I knew that as soon as I told that last story, Al would be gone forever. It was too emotional a moment to continue speaking, and so I stopped.

In a very real sense, though, this book is the seventh story. It is, after all, the last chapter—the last in the book and the one that sums up his life.

Al has been gone many years, but his legacy lives on. The Eicoff agency is one where people love to tell stories—not just about Al but about everyone (including me). It's a place where laughter is regularly heard. It's a business that prizes results above all else and is focused on delivering for clients year after year after. It's an agency that has never had a whiff of scandal and where everyone values ethical behavior. It's also a workplace where people feel free to express what they're feeling, where employees aren't constantly worried about losing their job, where they know that if they get their work done, they can leave at 5:00 and not worry that someone will say they're slacking off.

I ran the agency for a long time, and when he was alive, I always knew Al was there for me, even when we were arguing. Everyone looked to me for decisions as CEO, but I always could look to Al if necessary. It gave me a sense of security, and when he died, that security evaporated.

And yet, in a way, it didn't. I can still see Al as clear as day in my mind with his stained tie, askew toupee and ill-fitting suit, and all the memories and stories remain alive to me. And now, I hope they will also live for you.

94